Seeds, Trees, Branches, & Leaves

So eat more
with
Love
267-819-5487

Teresa Pearsall

AKA

Tree Pears

Continue to Sow the SEEDS
that bear HIS Fruits
Teresa Pearsall-Young

ISBN: 978-1-955312-08-0

Printed in the United States of America

Story Corner Publishing & Consulting, Inc.

1510 Atlanta Ave.

Portsmouth, VA 23704

Storycornerpublishing@yahoo.com

www.StoryCornerPublishing.com

Table of Content

Preface

Acknowledgments

Life Before HIM – Addictions
The First Time We Met
When A Mother Does Crack
A 'Dealt With' Situation
I Know What it Looked Like
Booty Call, Bounce!

Finding HIM – (HE Found Me)
A New Education
Before & After Him
That Old Coat
I Am Not Who I Used to Be
Who's Your Daddy
The Presents of His Gift
JOY (Jesus Oh Yes)
God is 24-7
Your Man is Mines

The Marriage – Till Death Do Us Part
My Husband
Alone
Addiction Came to Stay
Do Not Love Me to Death

Relationships
A Mother's Love
The Greatness of a Mother's Love
Before You Leap
A Valued Friend
Sister Kay

Observations
The Kitchen
The Voice Behind My Tears
Her Fur Coat
Like Tamar
What Does Your T-Shirt Say?

Vision
Unfinished
Vison Approved

Word Acapella
My Million is Waiting for Me
Call Me the Owner

NOW!

Teddy Bears & Balloons
Can I Take a Walk?
B.O.U.N.D - The Story of Angel
Why Am I The *B.O.M.B*?

Poem/Play – (R.I.P.) Rag in Progress

Preface

Seeds, Trees, Branches, & Leaves

Seeds – a source of development or growth *(merriam-webster.com, March 28, 2021)*

> *John 1:1 - In the beginning was the Word, and the Word was with God, and the Word was God*

A *seed* is the beginning of something that can be planted and grows once planted. From God's mouth, he began the world with a word. He spoke it, and it became. His word was the seed that was planted.

A seed is the equivalent to a word that is thought, that then turns into a word that is spoken and a sentence that is formed with and inclusive of the word. Therefore, a seed has been planted. That seed eventually grows into a tree that sprouts branches and leaves. *Read On.*

Trees - a woody perennial plant having a single usually elongate main stem generally with few or no branches on its lower part *(merriam-webster.com, March 28, 2021)*

> *Genesis 1:11 And God said, Let the earth bring forth grass, the herb yielding seed, and the fruit tree yielding fruit after his kind, whose seed is in itself, upon the earth: and it was so.*

A *tree* is a foundation that was grown from seed. It grew into a vital structure that sprouted branches and leaves.

Branches - something that extends from or enters a main body or source, a natural subdivision of a plant stem *(merriam-webster.com, March 28, 2021)*

> *John 15:2 Every branch in me that beareth not fruit he taketh away: and every branch that beareth fruit, he purgeth it, that it may bring forth more fruit.*

Branches are parts of a tree that grows out from the trunk or a bough and bears fruit or leaves.

Leaves – (definition) Foliage or a part of a book or folded sheet containing a page on each side *(merriam-webster.com, March 28, 2021)*

> *Revelations 22:2 In the midst of the street of it, and on either side of the river, was there the tree of life, which bare twelve manner of fruits, and yielded her fruit every month: and the leaves of the tree were for the healing of the nations.*

Leaves are colorful particles that sprout from the branches of a tree. Whether the branch loses the leaf or holds it, the tree will continue to create other leaves, to replace the lost leaves.

This book is my baby that has been in the birthing process far too long. My words are the seeds of the testimonies of my life before Jesus Christ and after giving my life to Jesus Christ.

The Tree that I speak of is me. I am the structure that God changed by giving me new life, with seeds to plant and words to express. The Branches are the many chapters of my life, each bearing many leaves. This book is my testimonies or stories in poetry, which I have named "*Stoetrys.*" They were not easy stories to tell, but the truth in all.

Because of God, I am a changed person. Never say never! Years ago, I spent time in many dark places before learning of the love of Jesus Christ and his kingdom. No one would have ever convinced me that 'this' is the place I would be in today and that I could be a light in a dark place. Please read through, and I hope you enjoy it. The following seeds for the next book are already planted, waiting to bring forth new Trees, Branches, and Leaves.

Enjoy!
Tree Pears

Luke 8:43-48 KJV

"And a woman having an issue of blood twelve years, which had spent all her living upon physicians, neither could be healed of any, came behind him and touched the border of his garment: and immediately her issue of blood stanched. And Jesus said, who touched me? When all denied, Peter and they that were with him said, Master, the multitude throng thee and press thee, and sayest thou, who touched me? And Jesus said, somebody hath touched me: for I perceive that virtue is gone out of me. And when the woman saw that she was not hid, she came trembling, and falling down before him, she declared unto him before all the people for what cause she had touched him, and how she was healed immediately. And he said unto her, Daughter, be of good comfort: thy faith hath made thee whole; go in peace. *(Biblegateway.com 4/18/2021)*

ACKNOWLEDGEMENTS

I would first like to acknowledge my Lord & Savior, Jesus Christ, whom with all things are possible.

I am a true *Rag in Progress*, as this was a work in progress, and long overdue. I gave my life to Christ in the year 2000, and I must tell you that turning back is not an option. My writings are my testimonies and observations, written in poetry & Stoetrys, which is a word I made up because some of the leaves are stories in poetic form. Through it all I must give God the Glory.

I would like to dedicate this book to my mother, Ludie Mae Pearsall, who went home to be with the Lord on April 21, 2018, after 91 years of being a blessing to her children and many she knew and loved. Mommy, I know you would be proud.

I also want to dedicate this book to my daughter, Syreeta Lynne Pearsall, whom I have never given up on. Although you face many struggles with illness, you are a survivor! You have endured and persevered and I love you forever and always. I am here for you. Keep on keeping on.

I want to shout out my niece, Shakira Bowman, aka Steddy Chanjin, for your fantastic artwork on my book cover. You captured everything that I wanted to portray. It was great working with you on this project. I love you, and I am proud of you and what's ahead for you.

To my Spiritual Parents, Apostle Timothy Brinson, and Pastor Michelle Brinson of

New Mercy Ministries, after 21 years of friendship and leadership, I thank you for never giving up on me.

You have always called me Daughter. Your mentorship has meant the world to me, I have grown so much because of your obedience and teaching of the unadulterated word of God. Remember that God did not change His mind about you.

To my family and associates, to the saved, newly saved, and been saved, and need to be saved again, I pray that my writings will bless you. They are based on my struggles and spiritual growth. Know that I am still learning, still getting fed, and striving to be better and more knowledgeable each day of the word of God and the Kingdom. This is a daily walk, but through faith, trusting and believing in Him, you can be healed, delivered, and set Free.

Love y'all,
Tree Pears

Life Before HIM- Addictions

The First Time We Met

The first time we met there was a deadly knock on the door of my soul.

Yet, excitedly, I opened that door, and there stood 'addictable.'

The substance, disguised as something so appealing, waited for my invitation.

It perceived me as being naïve, ignorant of the warning signs,

unknowing of the danger I placed myself in.

I heard myself saying, 'I'll try anything once', and with those few dangerous words,

Addiction entered my life.

The substance was so desirable, the habit held me liable for my actions.

At first, I thought this was only for the fun of it,

believing I could quit at any time, but as my addiction matured.

My excuse to use was that this pleasure would erase my pain, my fears, my issues, and my blues.

So, I opened my soul in acceptance, cradling the addiction as if it were my baby,

Looking for a temporary distraction from life's dissatisfaction,

But somewhere in the fog of things, I heard God ask, 'Why?'

He said, 'There are some things you just shouldn't try.'

Especially if they make you cry, or your bank account dry, friends and family say 'Girl, bye!'

Or give you the ultimate high because you will surely die!

Addiction looked me straight in the eye and dared me, it never cared for me.

Addiction played me like James Brown, singing 'Try Me'!

Addiction made me tell it, 'I love you', and it answered me, 'I know!'

Addiction invited a few of its friends, which were also unhealthy trends.

Addiction had me out of control; I was almost ready to sell my soul!

Addiction labeled me as predictable; it knew me as weak and addictable.

Addiction was always a special meeting to make me forget.

Yet, while forgetting, and fretting I was always regretting my actions.

Because suddenly you become more of what you were trying to forget before

More sick, more tired, more broke, more expired,

More suspect, more hateful, more undesirable, more ungrateful

Through my addiction, I was sleeping with the enemy!

When I realized my full potential, I woke up, and my soul cried out for help.

I could not take any more of me, so my mind and my soul demanded to be free.

Addictions are a trick of the enemy, not what God wanted you or me to be.

If you have an addiction that is hurting you or your family,

*please **CRY OUT FOR HELP**!*

You may be bound, but Jesus is bound to hear you.

The best addiction I ever had was to the word of God.

When A Mother Does Crack

This poem was written after being 7 years clean of abusing drugs.

I found this poem I wrote after looking through many writings I had authored and realized that God had been working on me for a long time, just like a simmering pot coming to a boil. I gave my life to Christ in the year 2000, and have many testimonies, but this is the one the Lord put on my heart to share, to help others break free from drug abuse or whatever fight they are fighting.
You can win!

Many years ago, I fought a terrible fight.
Used to run around hanging out at night.
Always had a shadow and was never alone.
Ghost chasing in the street, I should've been home.

I had a little girl; she was quite like me.
My life was too wild for her young eyes to see.
I started off teaching her the right way.
Needs of a fiend turned me on to the night's way.

I'd already lost the man that I had.
No kids of his own, but he was her dad.
He loved us to death, but I pushed him away.
I caused the man misery and much dismay.

What was thing that had me like that?
The substance I was smoking in a free- base bat.
I should have known better; I should have never started.
Once was not enough; I became weak hearted.

I started selling our things right out of the house.
My daughter didn't know what it was all about
At first, I sold my jewelry, then the VCR
I couldn't pay my mortgage and I lost my car

My daughter's young days were filled with gloom.

Why was the TV missing out of her room?
Dumb slave to the pipe, pushed my family apart.
I hated myself; slowly breaking their hearts.

Sucking up the clouds never made me forgot.
It was added self-destruction, I was more in debt.
Hiding from the dealer, you might think it's funny.
My daughter's life threatened if I didn't have his money.

I disappointed all of those who adored me.
Friends that I had stopped looking out for me.
Hitting rock bottom, I felt like a viper.
Two for five dollars, they were calling me a piper.

For my daughter it was time to do or die
I had to try; there was no more time to cry.
I learned to love myself, I knew I had potential.
For the life of my child, my recovery was essential.

Finally made up my mind, I had to move away.
Being freed from the elements that made me a slave.
Changed my way of living, had to make it better.
The least I could do, I knew I had to tell her that.

Starting all over again, is gonna be rough.
So rough, but we're gonna make it.
And then I told myself
Starting all over again, is gonna be hard.
But if I work with the Lord, I know I can make it.

After many years clean, thank the Lord I'm living
And all that I've got is all that I'm giving.
I raised my child with little help from a man.
I Praised the Lord, my crack life had an end.

My baby never hated me, now she loves me more.

To see a child in pain it hurts me to the core.
Mothers try to stay strong; you know drugs are wrong!
You worship the high, then your brain cells are gone.

A mother's love is more than food on the table.
It takes time and your brains to know that you're able.
Not just crack prone, you're the backbone in your family.
If it is God that you receive, you'll help others to believe.

My daughter makes me proud, as I've watched her grow.
Educating her mind; as I 'just say no!'
So many people hurt when a mother does crack.
I started all over and have never looked back.
For your Father knows the things you have need of before you ask him.
Matthew 6:8 KJV

A Dealt with Situation

I have a situation I must deal with I must try
It happened in the early years when I was getting high
A precious birdie told me when they were afraid to mention
She tried to tell me often, but I didn't give attention
He bothered her, he fondled her, but I tried not to hear it
I wanted to believe that all the kids had such great spirit
She told me once, she told me twice she didn't tell a lie
But I did not receive it then 'cause I was getting high
My precious birdie said to me this really messed her up
She felt that she had no one who'd protect her from the rough
She told the man who raised her, and he said he thought he knew
Well, if he knew of this bad thing why did he not subdue
The boy was not a man but what he did was to molest
He knew we thought him good, he put her silence to the test
What do you do when you've been robbed unknowing to your face?
I understand that now he's sheltered in a special place
The guilt that I still carry is so hard to be corrected
My precious birdie harmed, someone I thought that I protected
I am to blame, but loose the shame; I owe my birdie much
I hoped in life she'd never fight a hands unwanted touch
So, mothers, fathers, sinners, saints be watchful with your eyes
You cannot guard the one you love when you are getting high
The hurt I feel is there because I can't erase what's done
I love my birdie much and going forward we are one
You ask of my confession after hiding all these years
Not sharing holds me back and I need closure from these tears
I pray for birdie daily closing doors on problems past
I ask my God to heal, for her, my love forever lasts

I Know What It Looked Like

I know what it looked like, before in my past
In the heat of the night and the world of downcast
In my days I slept nights, in my nights I walked dazed.
After each hit, I took, I gave Satan the praise.

It looked like I would be sinning for life.
I would never amount to be somebody's wife.
Depressed from rejection, and real love restricted.
I was living outside in a prison convicted.

It looked like that I'd be alone and confounded.
I was not suicidal, but I was surrounded,
By demons of hopelessness, peace never lasted.
It wasn't the fear, I was foggy while blasted.

It looked like I'd prayed to an idol of drama.
Couldn't stand to live life without all the trauma.
Not a wonderful story for this baby's mama
Never thought in my future I'd be in a coma.

It looked like I lived my life having a ball.
Had a man on both sides, and one on call.
Had a 9-5 day job and nights 10 – 7
But those escapades couldn't get me to heaven.
Had a functional high and my dress was fly.
Had my nose in the air and the crystal pie.
I looked to be fine but when stopping to think.
The odors of my life were starting to stink.

I served the enemy and I served him well.
Head down, butt up, what a way to rebel
Not thinking that I may go straight to hell.
Why in this world would I continue to dwell?

Little did I know in the future of me.
Consuming the enemy's stale recipe
From my own drama would I try to flee
I almost couldn't be rescued, you see.

At this time, it looked like I wasn't too shrewd.
There were even the times that my acts were lewd.
But thank God my savior was taking me through.
Returning to be a good witness to you

I think of my past, but I live for my future.
As God strips the old and brings on the new
My thanks to my Lord for my life rearranged
I know what it looked like, but my life has changed.

Booty Call, Bounce!

I wrote this 'Stoetry' (a story in poetry) after hearing a message from a former pastor, called 'Church Off the Chain. Words matter. There are things that linger in our past that we may end as far as the action of it, but we may not be healed or delivered from the action. Some memories are like stones that lay heavy in your heart. Like kidney stones, they hurt while passing, but once dissolved, the pain is gone. We need to be purged of the past hurts. When we are out in the world, we as women accept things in our lives that we should not, making the men think that it is okay to treat us this way. I am not just speaking of the one-night stands, or even the tried it once, liked it and need to go back for seconds. I am speaking of those relationships that last some women for years. It is only a 'relationship' to us, not to the men. How many of you know what I am talking about? We set ourselves up to be letdown, because of acting out of desperation. We tell the man, I love you, and they say, I know! or thank you. Or 'awe, that's nice. Or if you love me, you should do whatever it takes to please me. We try to convince ourselves that it's better to have something, than nothing at all. Not true ladies. Do not play yourselves. I learned the hard way. And by the way, ladies, stop saying, 'I'll try anything once.' And stop doing that. It is some things we just shouldn't try. I know some of you have had a one-year booty call, but what about a seven year or better yet a thirty-year booty call, what!!! Oh yeah, it's possible, you will find me somewhere in between the one year and the thirty. Ladies that is a lot of time out of our lives to waste, for there to be no commitment. We cannot regain those years, and after each let down and heartbreak, we must start all over again, a little more bruised than before. Those years were painful for me, but today I can talk about it and I hope that I can help someone else be freed with my message of being delivered from the 'Booty Call'. Please read on while I share with you the stoetry of **'Booty Call, Bounce!'**

Booty Call, Bounce!

Ladies, can I minister, my intent is not sinister,

I hope you receive what I say

I'm speaking real life, now I'm somebody's wife,

my God told me to share this today

This healing began, with Church off the Chain,

thanks to Pastor I think I am free

I got married, thank God and we walked with the Lord,

we were blessed with a love you could see

I can speak of this lesson that I can now pass on,

the man of God helped to reveal

He turned on the lights to show 'Booty Call' nights had damaged my heart with a seal

It was back in my past, but the hurt could not last,

If I finally admitted my faults

Truths can now be unsealed, and my problem revealed,

as I came back to life with loves jolt

It was all in my past, but the heart break did last, until God came and covered me up

Hard addiction to cure, but the love is so pure,

when you drink from the Father's full cup

During Booty Call years,

I could not hide the tears as I labeled a few as 'good friends'

But no friend had my back, it was like a contract,

as the visits at night didn't end

Booty boasted to friends, quite a thing with the men,

but when darkness would turn into day

He was no booty novice, quickly gone without notice,

as his other life called him away

With such competition and some recognition,

Booty helped me move into a house

There was no guarantee,

Booty called to see me,

I should have never had reason to doubt

'Don't you love me? I said, as my face filled with dread,

because what was a mother to do?

I love nothing, he said except when we're in bed,

and don't act like you don't have a clue

Booty, please, that's not right, will you give up the fight,

this is not how a courtship should be

He said, 'girl don't pretend, just be glad we are friends',

'But you're nothing but booty to me'

Now wasn't I stupid, there was never a cupid to seal this thing with a sweet kiss

Now why would he jam me, I had not met his family,

And that's when reality hit

Well, Booty got engaged! I found out in a rage,

there was nothing to soften the blow

What he could not see yet was why I was upset, and why this thing affected me so

Yes, it cut like a knife, I was TKO'd twice, once again,

I was put to this shame

No more than a mistress in booty call distress, that was not a proud purpose to claim

One day God sat me down, he said cut the cord now,

before the cord cuts you in two

If you'd have been waiting, and not fornicating,

you would not be in this 'doo doo!'

Well, I closed my house down and turned my lights out,

I was no longer desperate you see

I got slapped in the head, it was Jesus, my dad, who had rescued and helped me to flee.

He said 'you are the best so don't settle for less',

you're better than those that you've had'

Reputation abused like some lover's old shoes,

as your worn to preserve the best pair

It became evident when my Jesus was sent,

to claim what was inside of me

Reconstructing my brain, I was being restrained, it was time that I let the flesh be

They say something is better than nothing at all, the devil is still a liar

Don't be fooled by the hype, it's the enemy's spite,

you need to let God take you higher

When you're sitting at home and you're all alone,

learn how to say no with the quickness

Do not pick up the phone, and don't open the door,

let the booty call go, it's a weakness

If your sweetness is weakness for reaching his peak-ness,

you know you must change up your style

Change your sweetness to meatless and phone calls repeat less,

and booties won't call for a while,

You know God's got your back as you fight this attack,

while you pimp smack the enemy down

I am speaking this thing, glorifying our king,

for our God is the teacher I found

Queens be a good thing to Kings with rings as best men step up to the plate

If expecting to marry, seek counsel and tarry take your vows,
then you can consummate
Thank God for the good thing, I have to prove nothing,
His love is for me and its free
Needed more than some cash, needed love and compassion,
and one to pray daily with me
Now I'm home all alone and I'm setting the tone,
And I'm waiting with dinner for two
When the phone rings at 10, It's my husband again, saying,
baby I'm ready for you

Finding HIM- (HE Found Me)

A New Education

I made it through high school and had some college
I've always yearned to acquire more knowledge
I'd learned just enough, what I thought was right
To handle my business and make it through life

I worked through the years, but it was my rule
To stay fresh in the mind and return to school
Each year that I grew with fates preparation
God's plan for me was a new education

Very street smart, I thought I was hip
Life's merry go round took me on a wild trip
The drama, the headaches, the negative beings
The issues, the threats, and the afterthought fleeing

But one day God stopped me, He said it quite clear
'You may as well stop all your running my dear!'
Achiever, crowd pleaser, but always alone
'You know that God's calling, now come to the zone!'

I entered the zone, but not sure of the lesson
I learned that I always had God in possession
Through all of my sinning, I could not hide
'Cause God was within me, yes God was inside

He taught me a new thing through His Holy word
This teaching far better than any I'd heard
He fed the Apostle for those who assembled
His message through Pastor would cause me to tremble

Blessed with His anointing and full of His zeal
The knowledge I've gained as a Christian is real
I am strengthened, so new and so wonderfully blessed
I praise the almighty and yearn His caress

Who would have thought that today I'd be ministering?
With growing obedience to God, I am winning
When I hit Heaven's station, my last graduation
I'll have earned all degrees in my new education

Praise God! Thank you, Father, Son & the Holy Spirit

Before Him

I'd walk around with my head hanging down
My mood could be judged from miles around
Folks would say, girl, you look so mean
I did not feel this, but it is what was seen

They told me I wore my pain on my sleeve
My hurts were well hidden, it's what I believed
I thought that you always should dress to impress
But my garb reflected that I was depressed

My colors were dark, black, grays and browns
The earth tones would blend me right into the ground
My outfits reflected my soul's distress
I had not acknowledged the Jesus caress

The colors I wore were all colors of dirt
It was seldom I put on a bright dress or shirt
I took on the pain of myself and of others
But this was before Jesus Christ I discovered

After Him

My mindset has changed with the lessons I've learned
My lessons in life have now taken a turn
I am thanking the Lord for bringing me out
I now celebrate JOY without a doubt

My prayer life has changed, and my wardrobe has brightened
When folks see me coming, they're no longer frightened
They want to know what my new glow is about
I've met the Lord Jesus; He's bringing me out.

It's not just the clothes but He's said no more hiding

He's changed my esteem and He's always providing
Although what I need is not my first desire
Absorbing the word brings the Holy Ghost fire

Humbly I walk with my head held up high
I smile and greet people as they pass me by
They do not know why but they always smile back
The smile's a reflection of Jesus attack

I've grown and improved with His love reflection
There's no longer room for the devil's infection
No more sadness and worrying, both actions are sinful
My attitudes changed; I've accepted Him in full

Now souls that will see me will first see my glow
He's blessed me and now His anointing must flow
For a life changing method, He's the best medicine
Wish I'd known Him before, now I'm blessed after Him.

That Old Coat

I walked by that old closet, with my old coat hanging there
The closet a reminder of the life I used to wear
The coat had dust and smelled of old, but still a memory
Of all things I used to do that lived inside of me

The spirits wrestled with me, and reminded of what was
Thoughts and evil memories struck like lightning from above
The staleness in the closet was the enemy's cologne
I had to shut the door when Satan's essence filled the room

The coat, too large, too small, thank God the coat no longer fit
My promise to the Lord was that no compromise, no split
The time has come to bury it, this coat's life has expired
The coat can burn with Satan, 'cause it's time to say, You're Fired!

Can't hold on to those memories, and compromise His name
There' nothing there to do me good, but bring me further pain
Whatever needs to go, be gone, the closet will be cleaned
I have a brand-new wardrobe and it shows my life redeemed

I Am Not Who I Used to Be

Years ago, when I was me
It wasn't for the world to see
The wild and sometimes hidden being
Most actions a forbidden scene

Well as I grew, I learned, not loved
Of other sins I'm not proud of
My world was me under a glove
The glove a mask to cover up

The sins I knew they were not rare
Yet some sins caused me not to care
I lived two worlds which was not fair
I'd never let you meet me there

A time of hurts and secret rains
And all for love I did not gain
A cushion softening the pains
I'd choose another road, insane

Of many things I was ashamed
But I would pay a price for fame
I reckoned others knew my game
I wished they didn't know my name

But God is good and what you see
Is not the one I used to be
I'm no longer ashamed of me
I've changed, thank God, and now I'm free

I now can say when of my past
I'm glad my era did not last
I had a ball and had a blast
But slowly I was dying fast

My life has changed because of God
The raunchy road no longer trod
He said to me I will provide
If you reveal the God inside

No longer do I live to die
I die to live and prophecy
My past is now a world gone by
And Jesus is the name I cry

I've been reborn, it shows in me
I'll not turn back from me I'm free
I'm not the one I used to be
It's me for God and God for me

Who's Your Daddy?

In life there are many fathers.
Our Father who art in heaven
Our biological father and
Our spiritual father
Our father who art in heaven is
The founder and creator of the universe
He has allowed our creation by conception
Thru our biological parents.
Our father who art in Heaven was always there,
But the first daddy we've ever met was our biological dad
His role was to raise us, and
Watch us grow and teach us of
Our father who art in heaven

Many of us do not know who our biological father is
Our spiritual father then becomes our father figure
Knowing our father who art in heaven
Has led us to a Spiritual Father
That teaches us of our Father who art in heaven
Just as some biological fathers do when they are in our lives
Spiritual fathers spread themselves amongst many families,
But the families know who their spiritual father is
And the purpose he serves

We must thank God for our spiritual Fathers
Many of us know our spiritual daddy
Better than we know our biological daddy
Because of our spiritual fathers
We know more about Christ, and more about life,
We have been schooled, therefore we have learned

We pray for our spiritual fathers
And ask that they continue to teach us,
Speak to us, preach to us, and mentor us
Continuing as a fivefold ministry
Letting us know who our Daddy is
Who's your daddy?
In the Kingdom, it's God
On earth, it's your friend, your teacher, your Pastor, your Apostle
Your Spiritual Daddy

The Presents of His Gift

God's gift to Mary, was a gift to the earth
Not conceived but begotten, He arrived through birth
To save all people, or those who believed
In a Bethlehem manger, a life was received
The presents of His gift made a blind man see
Jesus died for our sins to save you and me
The presents of His Gift too numerous to mention
It's the Word in the bible if you pay attention
Endurance, Redemption, and even His Anointing

Receiving His Power, there is no disappointing
He will shield & protect, and He lives life through you
Give Glory to His name, and He gives you Halleluiah
Builds your Faith and Belief in the Body of Christ
He gave you all breath with His Gift of Life
Caring, concern, deliverance, and Favor
Straight from the Bible it is the Word we savor
He gives you recovery and reconciliation
He does a new thing and provides restoration
He provides a Way Out, grace & mercy & Freedom
Jesus is the name; you can call Him when you need Him

Gives the power of Healing & God's Intercessors
With Your Praise to the Lord, He destroys the Oppressor
Gives you humans and Angels, & Help from the Lord
He is the Almighty Word, Sharp Like a sword
Prophecy, and Victory, still he gives you Tribulations
Makes you understand why we all need Salvation
God gave us Jesus, He is Christ our Savior
Joy, Love & Peace are the gifts that he gave you.
Worshipping His name, you receive the Holy Spirit
With the gift of Tongues, speak to Him until He hears it.
His gifts exude His Presence and your spiritual growth

When you shout, feel the power of Holy Ghost
Gives a mansion in Heaven and abundant life
When you live for Him, He will do you right
Eternity in Life is the Gift that he promised
If we gave our life to Christ...whether happiness or conflict
Wealth provided for the kingdom, from the Father & Son
I have 99 problems but His Gift ain't one

JOY (Jesus Oh Yes)

Jesus
It is you that I owe the glory
The omnipotent master of divine humanity
The son of God
The shedder of the blood
Oh, what a wonder is He
What a sacrifice He made
He bore the weight of the cross on his back
With nails in hand as the blood trickled down
As Mary cried, my son, my son!
As the mourners could not fathom this tragedy
He died and rose again
As the stone was removed and He was not there
And the mourners exclaimed
With Joy, He has risen
He died for our sins
But He has resurrected
And we have
Jesus, Oh yes
We have JOY!

God Is 24/7

FYI, For your information
God is not a one-minute man
However, In 60 seconds,
He can change the world
God is not a sixty-minute man
He will bless you when He is ready
God does not start to jump at 1:00 a.m.
He is not the party pooper,
He is the celebration
God is not bi-weekly,
nor is He semi-annual
He is not the 1st or the 15th
But on the 1st and the 15th,
* you will say, Thank God!*

God is not a 9 to 5, or a 3 to 11,
* or the midnight shift*
God is not just breakfast, lunch or dinner
He is definitely not a late-night snack,
but you should thank God for every morsel
God is not just king for a day

He is not just to be celebrated on December 25, or New Year's Eve
God is not just in the month of February, like black history
God is not leap year, but how far will you leap for Him
God is not the new millennium,
nor is he 01-01-01, God is the One

If you fast, it does not mean, no God
God will never say no to you

God is not the summer, winter, spring or fall
God is not spring break, but He is all seasons

God is not an appointment to think about keeping
God is not to be included in your schedule, He is the schedule
God is not rush hour, nor is he peak time
But God says, reach my peak
God is not a chance you take

But with God, you'll have a chance
God is not limited to 2 per customer There is never a limit on God
God is not a ski trip in the mountains
But He will take you higher, if you want to go

God isn't just a few minutes of your time, God is time
He is the seconds, the minutes, the hours, and the days
God is the best thing since sliced bread
God broke the bread and multiplied it
God is your first and your last breath
God is the morning, noon, and night
God is from dusk 'til dawn
God is from sunrise to sunset
God is the North, South, East, and the West

God does not hate, for God is love
God is the universal mail man
Be it rain, snow, sleet or hail
He will deliver, he will not fail
God is like 7-11, He is always open
God is forever, God is 24-seven

Glory be to God!
The Father, the Son
And The Holy Ghost.

Your Man is Mines

I was with Your man last night, as I gave in to sweet surrender
That man that you called yours had me spellbound, with all His splendor
I tried to pull away, but his calm presence pulled me in
He called my name so sweet, my spirit tingled deep within

Oh God, how soothing was His touch, a sensitive caress
His cleansing glow inside, it stirred a healing in my mess
I laid with him, I slept with Him, we prayed between the sheets
I wept with Him, I laughed with Him, the time we spent was sweet

The overflow, the afterglow, there was no guilt or shame
He is your man, He told me so, but yet He called my name
Hurt hearts have claimed Him as the one who fills a room with love
His consecrated power soars like eagles flying above

He can hold you in His arms or sooth your pain where you may stand
Leave your wound-up soul unbound, to speak a word whenever you can
He's my man, my friend, my pal, and he's your man, we know it's true
I was with Him just last night, and as you mentioned, weren't you?

I hope you didn't mind, but in the morning, we had brunch
I had the nerve and gall to invite our man back for lunch
His presence was so strong, He went quite well with my late snack
As His spirit called the doves and knocked the enemy on His back

I praised His holy presence, and I thanked Him for last night
The prayers that I sent up have called Him heavy to my plight
My man, your man, her man, his man, a man we all can claim
He's got the whole world in His hands, so holy, Jesus is His name

He is the one man we all share, no envy in this space

We take him with us daily and forever seek His face
Jehovah, Jesus, EL Shaddai, the names are all for one
I pray and tears of Joy I cry, they're for the Holy Son

I know that your man loves me, and my love is not absurd
I shared your man last night and once again I heard His word
We boast and brag of Him that he's the best lover around
Jesus is that man and by His blood, we're heaven bound

The Marriage- Til Death Do Us Part

The Marriage- Till Death Do Us Part

(I was married from September 28, 2002 through October 29, 2009. We tried to make it work, however many spirits got in the way as you will see with the next few poems. We were not equally yoked. We had love for each other, and I was happy to finally be getting married, but it was not the way God intended it to be. During his last days, he made his peace with God. I was with him until the end. When he transitioned, he appeared relieved to be free of pain, suffering no more).

My Husband

When my husband walked through the door.
After a hard day's work, it was confirmed. I was so happy to see him.
I missed him while he was gone, in the beginning.
I always prayed for his safe return.
I asked God to protect him and return him home safely.
I assured him when he arrived that I did love him.
At that time, I was glad that we took our vows.
I loved him, he loved me.

The look on his face, never showed regret for the vows, we took, the vows we changed.
For richer or poorer, for sickness and in good health,
We removed the 'poorer and sickness' from our vows.
But we lived in sickness and at times poorer, which showed us you cannot change Gods vows.
When my husband walked in, he said 'I love you, I am glad I'm home'.
'Come here honey, give me a kiss.' He would speak lovingly.
Hey Boo, Heyyyyy!

I thought that no one or nothing could separate us.
That God would always keep us together.
That he was for me and I was for him
His growth in the Lord was astounding, so I thought.
I was still growing as well, learning Christ in a new way.
I was so happy for his new life, that I could not see the forest for the trees.
I thought he was new and different that he was changing, for the better

He was still getting his house in order, getting a makeover, being renovated,
His value had appreciated, so I thought, as had mines.
He was my asset.

I always wanted to protect my assets and my values and my interests.
My husband was mines to protect, so I thought.
I thought everything was fine until I started discovering all the hidden agendas
That he did not want me to see.
I uncovered them on my own, like Dick Tracey, or the FBI/ CIA as he called me.
What kind of fool did he thinks I was?
The smoking, the drinking, the parties when I was gone.
He was sick, and getting sicker, but disregarded doctors' orders.
People used to ask what was wrong with him, I said; 'Everything!'

Taking medicine on one day and drinking on the next. He was his own party.
He was his own destruction. The man I married had left. The man he already was, had returned.
I tried to help him, I tried to love him, I tried to keep him.
The devil wanted him; God wanted him more.
He flirted with God and loved on the devil.
I loved him anyway, I wish I could have loved him more.
My Husband Died on 5/16/2016, at the young age of 63.

Alone

In this marriage, we're together, but sometimes I'm so alone
I look at him and wonder why I love him to the bone
Committing to relationship, it's now a painful love
And as I cry, I blame it on the man of God above

I know my husband loves me but there's so much he can't see
The growing pains are mental, and directly hurting me
I've told him of the damage, but he can't accept the truth
I've spoken it back and forward, what more do I need for proof

He entertains old demons, while not letting go of God
The battle is within me, just to keep him on God's squad
When will he allow the Father to reverse and break the mold?
He must learn to hear God's voice and to practice self-control

He must release his mind so he can be a kingdom ruler
Train his body to perform so he'll become his own home schooler
I can't take it, but I have, said I love you, sometimes not
I have stayed but want to go; love's remorse is what I've got

Sure, he is a man of God, but his body needs some healing
I'm trying to hold on, to keep that same old married feeling
People think we are so happy when they view us as a team
They don't notice there are branches slowly falling off my tree

Without God I could not do this, He's the only one who cares
Even though my Hubby brags and boasts of all the things we share
Thank you, God, you are my pillar and you've even been my post
That is why I do commit to loving you and you the most

The tears, released, expressed, held back, what do I have to gain
Wet if I cry, dry if I hurt, the sadness is dry pain
I know I vowed to love you for better or for worse,
I'll be the first to say it, this was nothing I rehearsed

For sure, I should have waited, planned it for another season
For legal sex we married, which was surely the wrong reason
'Can't we remain good friends?', that is what I should have said
But I tried to do the right thing in the eyes of God instead

But God didn't say get married, did not say to tie the knot
He really said to wait my dear, be blessed with what you've got
I listen closer now and as I do a real review
I blame it all on me; I am the stronger of the two

My man, my love, my life, and who I greet when I come home
How do I let him know that I am feeling so alone?
I'll always chase the demons that surround him in his head
They have to go, or I'll be out, before I end up dead.

Addiction Came to Stay

Addiction walked beside us, holding my partner's hand like a best friend forever.
It was Invisible, but I could see it, living through him, making its presence felt.
Treating me like the other woman, succeeding at making our lives miserable.
When we took our vows, addictions were at the altar.
When we went to counseling, addictions sat down alongside of us.
I begged addictions to leave my partner alone, as the addictions were
Like an unwanted guest that wouldn't go home
But addictions held on to my partner's hand, they were so in love.
My partner thought he couldn't live without them,
as the stench exuded from his skin,
his morning promise was 'I'll never do that again.
Of course, until the next time.

He wanted to give up without even trying,
addictions didn't care that he was dying,
I heard him crying, in need, wanting each substance in greed.
Still not believing it was such a negative seed, that he was sowing into himself.
Question - How do we help our loved ones evict the addiction, the unwanted substances?
Addiction comes in all shapes, sizes, colors and creeds,
cigarettes, coke, pills, alcohol and weed!
Meant to destroy a person in need who feels there is no higher power.
So, the addiction becomes the minute and the hour,
and you watch as it devours the lives, making them think they can't survive,
telling addictions "I'm lost without you," like CeCe.
With captives needing an excuse to be bound,
they find reasons not to put addictions down.
They may think this is a way to play, and they'll be fine one day,
but addiction came to stay.

Addiction is a challenge to your loved one's conviction,

and deliverance cannot be temporary,
It's necessary.
For many, withdrawal is scary, but cleansing is a correction,
because addiction is an infection,
and there has to be a rejection in the person's mind and
their desire must become a need to leave addictions behind.
Rest in Peace - To my husband

Do Not Love Me to Death

As I watch my man smoking his cigarette,
I find it hard to breath.
In my own environment
My man is killing me softly.
By secondhand smoke
As he blows smoke out of his mouth,
He says, 'I love you, honey!'
'I'd kill a nigga over you!'

I try to believe him, and I do,
But he is killing me!
As I look at his twisted lips, his glassy eyes,
And watch him cough from the smoke.
I just want to scream!

It is hard to say, 'I love you!' back.
When I know my health is at risk
'Baby, I love you to death!' he says,
With sincerity in his eyes and a cigarette in his hand
Unfortunately, the words are literal,
What do I do, but love him back and try to avoid the smoke?
I must breathe to live,
So, I try not to choke, this is an unfunny joke.

But the words I have said.
Were as if I had never spoke them.
What kind of love should I show for him?
Do I continue to beg for his life?
Am I wrong for doing this, as a wife?

I am seeing the years flash by
As I wait for him to get better or at least try.
How long should I wait, anticipate?
As he says he loves me so
I am still waiting for the love to show.
Trying to save my breath.
Love me if you must, honey.
But please,
Do not love me to death!

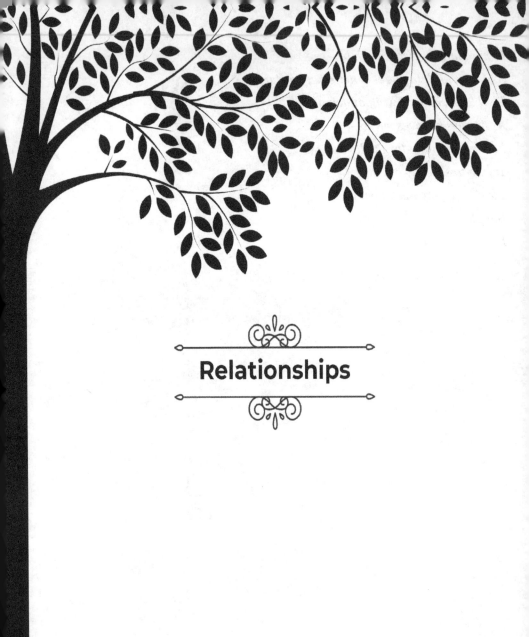

Relationships

A Mother's Love

A Mother's Love
Is like a summer scene on a backyard porch
With the sun shining and a cool breeze blowing
You want to embrace the moment
And pray that it never ends

A Mother's Love
Is just like a serving of
***Her** fried chicken, a slice of **her** carrot cake*
*And a pitcher of **her** southern tea*
It is to die for and to live for
And you just got to have it

A Mother's Love
Will teach you from birth about
Life, growth and survival
She's been there, done that
Got the T-shirt and the cap
She will not want you
To make the mistakes she's made
Or even to pay the price she's paid
She'll want you to have it made in the shade
With a glass of lemonade!

A Mother's Love
Will want to
Protect you at any cost
She will always be your mama,
As you pay the cost to be the boss

A Mother's Love

Will show you

How to love another man, woman, child, or friend

How to love yourself and not to depend

On promises, lies, or weaknesses of others

A Mother's Love is the truth!

A Mother's Love

Will give you spiritual guidance and strength,

It will point you in God's direction

A Mother is God's right-hand man

Just like the love of God,

A Mother's Love is unconditional,

She will love you when others just can't

If you think nobody loves you,

Look for your Mama and look for God

A Mother's Love

Will remind you of what your Mama said

Give Mom her flowers now, don't wait until she's dead.

Her love is your support system, a shoulder to lean on

She's your mentor and motivator

In your accomplishments, you may not please a crowd

But somehow you can always make your Mama proud

A Mother's Love

Has the spirit of discernment

A Mother's instinct and

Intuition is better than any crystal ball or psychic,

You better listen to your Mama

Your Mama will travel your journey

While you take your own trip

And when you return,
She'll be waiting for you
And your luggage
At the at the end of that road

A Mother's Love
Teaches necessity, and the
Important things a child must know
If necessity was the Mother of invention
The invention of a Mother was a necessity
Who else would have known how to nurture you or me?

A Mother's Love
Will love her children and they will always be her babies
A Mother will love her babies and they may not be her children
A Mother's baby is whatever she wraps her arms around
And nurses to growth and maturity, a son or daughter, a plant, a book,
A casserole, a business, a community, or a congregation
The term multi-tasking also means Mother tasking

A Mother's Love
Will carry dreams and visions
Of the future, setting examples for you to follow
A Mother's Love has a big role to play
In giving birth to contributions of the universe
It's not nice to fool Mother Nature, and
You better not fool with your Mama

A Mother's Love
Should be celebrated, honored and cherished
With hugs, smiles and laughter and good times
A Mother's happiest time is
Spending good times with her family or families

A Mother's Love

Is the glue that holds a family together

There's no end to the territory that can be covered with A Mother's Love

And when you have excelled because of your Mama

And return to your old neighborhood

Remember the best hood in the

Whole wide world is the hood called Motherhood.

The Greatness of a Mother's Love

A Mother's Love, sometimes misunderstood
But the greatest hood to hangout in is Motherhood.
A Mother's love has a voice, that speaks volumes.
It is soft, loud, calm, stern, warm, and emotional,
A Mother's love has strength, it's devotional.
A Mother's love grows Just like a mustard seed,
Planted! Like a TREE sprouting branches with many leaves
A Mother's love will possibly smother you,
but she prays that God will always cover you
A Mother's love claims you as her baby,
You'll never hear her call you mommies maybe

From birth through life, her instinct will protect you,
her plans are never to reject or neglect you
Mother's love will inspect you, there are goals she expects of you,
and at the right time she'll still respect your privacy.
A Mothers love is a kind of love, that's great, and kind,
a love to celebrate, that many pray to find
Her love, like agape, is unconditional
Her love, like tough love, will whip you,
read you, then hug and kiss you,

When you're gone, she'll always miss you.
A Mother's love is free,
doesn't need to be earned but may be yearned by the mother-less
A Mother's Love becomes a surrogate for others in need,
for those who can't breed, or have no one to nurture their seed
A Mother's love masters mother fathering when daddy's not bothering
A Mother's love is our back up plan, a safety net, nice home,
a delicious meal, or in most cases, a quick loan,
that's keeping it real
We fear Jesus and a mother's love the same,
trying to hide our shame when they are not to blame

A Mother never forgets when she birthed you,
but never wants to know someone has hurt you
A Mother's love knows when you're lying, cannot bear when you're crying,
or know her child's dying
A Mother's love gives you hope, making you laugh at her unfunny jokes
Being covered by a mother's love is a benefit, lifetime insurance,
teaching patience & endurance, combined with blessed assurance

A love, so Grand and Great, that Moms-To-Be can hardly wait,
to share love they acquired, a love their mother inspired.
Our first mother, Eve, was the mother of ALL living,
granted greatness in earth, God gave the gift that kept on giving
God prophesied Sarah would be mother of nations,
she laughed, but bore Isaac, which became generations

Mary, God chose her, to birth the gift of Salvation, she mothered Jesus 'til 33,
He became our Lord & Savior
A mother's love cries, bleeds, hurts, grieves,
learns, yearns, teaches & preaches, discovers, recovers,
and prays at length, turns from worries & weakness to richness & strength
A Mother's love is so precious but when she's gone,
she leaves memories, and legacy, her spirit carries on
Her love is an asset with a return on investment,
when her love is rewarded, happiness is her present
Mother's Love presents greatness in every way,
not just for today, but always, every day
From Mothers to Grands, and Mothers-To-Be,
and mothers who love us spiritually,
becoming a mother of greatness and pleasure is a gift from God we will always
treasure.

Before You Leap

We let go of our seed, once they are grown
They are older and have ideas of their own
We want the best, but we can't make their plans
We can't pick their friends, choose their woman or man

We sometimes wish we could raise their child
Then we say go home, don't come back for a while
We ask you to tell us when things get rough
In the real world we know that life can get tough

Be cautious of life while you're having fun
There are storms and tornadoes that hide behind the sun
Do not be surprised when the rain showers come
Each puddle is different for everyone

Can we build your house, bake your bread?
Sweep your floor, make your bed
Dress you up, and rub your head
Plan your life, no tears would be shed

Would you love us more or love us less?
Would you dress your change or change your dress?
Would you follow our rules, or put them on the shelf?
Would you repeat my mistakes or repeat yourself?

Do a double take, please don't repeat my mistakes
Would you follow our rules and participate?
Please stay in prayer don't just get by
Please check yourself don't live a lie

And know your mate don't lay down so fast
If you put them first, do not put me last
If they put you last, you may need me first

No one can quench your mother's thirst

She will hold you still and wipe your tears
She will feel your pain and calm your fears
My daughter, my child, My son, my gem
My prayers will cover you, head to hem

I love you child but live your life
We try to survive with minimal strife
Whatever God shows you in your sleep
Look ahead to the future before you leap

A Valued Friend

Through thick and thin, we've hung together
The bond is strong, the trust forever
From young to old, we've come along
Through trials and trails, remaining strong
We've made mistakes.
We've bumped our heads
But blessed we are, cause we're not dead
Some lessons hard, but we still learned
To make attempts for what we 've yearned
We've yearned for life, for what wealth brings
We owe ourselves those precious things
Your value 's priceless as a gem
Because you are my valued friend
We may not see each other much
But near or far our hearts still touch
You've never asked for anything
You've held your own through everything

At times it seemed the rain just poured
We overcame and then ignored
The negatives that had us bound
We saw roadblocks but walked around
We've been through things that we both know
But through it all we dared to grow
We had to keep the Lord in mind
We kept our faith with strength combined
Our children call us family
And that's the way it ought to be
They celebrate our long friendship
They never saw our value stripped
Through joy and pain through thick and thin
We keep in touch until the end
Sisters for life, through thick and thin

You'll always be my valued friend
In dedication to my dear friend for life, Cysvera Edwards
(Rest in Peace Dennis Edwards- Her only child and son).

Sister Kay

The next day was her last day
She had no way of knowing it
There was love in her heart and
She thought that she was showing it
There was anger in his mind
All the while he was storing it
She tried to be his help
But slowly he was losing it

We'll never understand
As it was not her time to go
We thought her world was grand
Not the tragedy that showed
But the thing we couldn't see
Was why he couldn't 'just say no'?
Her spirit has been set free
Leaving still her spirit's glow

Was he a coward or a man?
What demon made him take her life?
We must be careful of our words
As we want to stay in Christ
This tragedy so senseless
A loss that cuts just like a knife
We must pray for the survivors
That they live and do what's right

Even if the wrong's not right
Every victim needs a prayer
As we speculate and wonder

Knowing that we weren't there
As we wish it never happened
What we must all keep in mind
As the dancer and the one that Praised
Sister Kay was sweet and kind

Dedicated to Sister Kay, who was sadly and senselessly killed in a murder suicide.

Observations

The Kitchen

The kitchen is
the heart of the household
The place where stories are told around Jell-O molds
The place where many preparations are made
For Thanksgiving, bar-b-cues, and marmalade
Stirring lemonade so we can sit in the shade
Making wedding plans, mothers' orders obeyed

In the kitchen is where we
Plan for college as we look ahead
We even plan for newborns or to bury our dead
Under pressure tears may be shed
As we straighten the kinky hair on our heads

In the kitchen reunions are planned
As preserves are canned
Jokes are told as lives unfold
Tales are spun as hearts are won
History is shared as souls are borne

In the kitchen pies are baked
No shake and bake, but I helped
As babies cried, while chicken is being fried
As we invite folks to stay
Sit around the table playing cards all day

In the kitchen we tell lies,
No, tall tales while juice drinking
Doing homework, Table thinking
Who stole the cookie from the cookie jar?

Marinade the steak and fill up the spice bar
The heart of the house is the kitchen
Where plans are made as we drink lemonade
And the future is planned
As the rest of the house is reserved
In a jar, waiting to get old, Like preserves
In the kitchen

The Voice Behind My Tears

So many times, you've seen me cry
As droplets come and fill my eyes
Responding to an urgent call

Emotions touched, a nerve that's tapped
And sometimes there's no holding back
The tears become a waterfall.

My tears may fall like stormy rain
I cry without the sound of pain
But who shall judge me when I cry?

Some tears replace the verbal sound
Or a connection that's been found
Some tears will end a day gone by

My tears may be a sentiment
For thoughts that may be heaven sent
Because I'm filled with thoughts of Him

Those tears that say that I am new
And I am that because of you
Express my holiness to them

For if you're hurt, I feel your pain
And if you're blessed, I'm strong again
My tears reflect your mirrored view

Who can interpret all my tears?
That show my gratitude or fears
And tears that show I love you too

Can you dissect my tears today?

Has pain or gain come across my way?
What of the tears that you can't see?

Yes, what about my silent drops
With golden silence, voices stopped
When somethings died inside of me

Sometimes there is no other way
To thank the Lord as we do pray
The tears are welcome signs of praise

Some people sing, some speak in tongue
I worship Him with shout and song
And tears that show He's blessed my days

My tears may show that I've been through
But I'm saved now because of you
Inside of me the tears are store

The tears I have for love, affection
Outweigh those for sympathy, rejection
For tears of sorrow there's no reward

GOD catches the drops for the tears you've shed
He nurtures your thoughts for His vision, no dread
He knows all your tears whatever they're for

Whatever there for, don't hold them back
That may be the way to rebuke an attack
To voice the tears deep in your core

Her Fur Coat

As she walked out of the door of her beautiful home
She secured her sunglasses on her face
Looking like a million on the outside
Feeling indebted on the inside
She tightened her fur coat around her
So soft and furry, big enough to hide
The hurt and abuse underneath it all
To look at her, she would be the envy of many
To know her, most would never want to be in her shoes

Her sunglasses would hide the pain in her eyes of an unhappy relationship
Her fur coat would hide the bruises and scars of abuse
But mainly it would cover up the hurt inside of her
Knowing that you love someone who won't love you
The way you want to be loved

She walks across the street to her new car
It's so beautiful, plush, jazzy, sparkling
Yet another trinket to cover up what is not there
Or should I say, who is not there when he needs to be there,

Oh, how he needs to be there!
She can ride off into the sunset
But the place called 'there' is someplace
That always makes her come back home
Many times, she has decided to run,
Flee, take off and not look back
But she just can't leave the things,
The stuff, the treasures, the masquerade
Her biggest treasure that she has lost is, Herself

Her children are beside her,
As she ushers them into the back seat
Dressed so perfect and neat
Oh, how she loves them
Places no one above them
Can always rely on them to love mommy
For them she will always be Mommy
But she asks, what about me
Do I take the children and flee?
As she begs 'Lord please rescue me'

Her soul is abused, and her body's been used
Buried under the fur, and the car, and the fine things
The man she loves unconditionally, who covers up the wrong
By rewarding her with gifts, just a momentary lift
She asks, 'Lord why am I fighting to keep this?'

She believes that one day the madness will stop
And they will live happily ever after
She can wear the fur coat in the cold winter months
But until things change, what will be
The cover for the cold nights in the summer

Like Tamar

Who Was Tamar?

Samuel 2:13

Tamar, sister of Absalom, half-sister to Amnon were three of King David's 20 children. Tamar, the only known daughter & Absalom had the same mother.

Tamar was identifiable by her robe as a virgin maiden.

Amnon desired her, and His servant & cousin, Jonadab, devised a plan to have King David to invite Tamar to help care for Amnon in sickness.

Amnon was only sick by his lust for Tamar, his sister.

When she arrived and got close, he raped her, then hated her. Tamar tore her robe and wailed in the street upon departure, indicating that she had been violated.

When Absalom found out, he bade her to keep it a secret.

When King David found out he was enraged but did nothing.

Two years down, Amnon was deceived, just like Tamar, into attending a sheepshearing event, and was struck down & slain by his brothers from Absalom's order, to avenge Tamar's defilement.

In this biblical story it tells of deception, trickery, rape, scandal, embarrassment, anger, revenge, murder, mourning and secrets within the family.

Like Tamar

Tricked *– Like Tamar,*

Have you ever been lured by a familiar face?

Invited to a house you thought a safe place?

An act in your life that you cannot erase

Someone summoned, so cunningly, asking 'Will you please, help me?'

Innocently, you came, as you were called by name,

But suddenly, the request had changed, and realization hit,

Someone Tricked You!

Ambushed *- Like Tamar,*

Have you ever been invited by someone who was your family or their friend?

Who offered rewards, or gifts, if certain meetings you would attend?

Were you asked to serve someone dinner, but found the food was not the reason you entered?

You were willing, thought you were caring, but food was not the menu they were sharing.

When asked you did not hesitate, so happy to participate, did not want to be late.

Once arrived, you discovered too late, there was no way of escape, when realization hit,

Someone Ambushed You!

Molested - *Like Tamar,*

Someone could have been Cousin Steve or Uncle Jack,

Or maybe the boys that live out back

You were innocent and unsuspecting, but devastation you were not expecting

The idea of it so unnerving, you were young and possibly a virgin

Someone's sins of lust and desire caused someone else to conspire, to abuse an innocent soul.

A plan of deception, hidden, just to pluck a flower, forbidden, while your story should not be

told. When Realization hit

Someone Molested You!

Ashamed - *Like Tamar*

By someone's actions, you were defamed, unspeakable!

Deflated, heartbroken and ashamed. Despicable!

A lascivious act, someone caused it

But hated you now, blamed you for the fault of it

You cried, 'Please, no! But someone still pursued in this

Someone, determined to act in lewdness when realization hit:

Someone Ashamed You!

Raped - *Like Tamar*

You walked in pure & innocent, but were not protected

Now scarred for life, imminent danger not detected

Deflowered, mocked, trashed, and rejected

You know who your someone is, and dream of revenge

Someone's related or maybe a friend, but family secrets lie within, but when realization hits.

Someone Raped You!

What Does Your T-Shirt Say?

*Genesis 35:2 - Then Jacob said unto his household, and to all that were with him, put away the strange gods that are among you, and be clean, and change your **garments***

The type of garment I want to talk about today is a T-shirt.

I've been doing a survey recently.

I don't want people to think I'm strange,

but I've been reading females T-shirts,

as I see them being worn in the streets.

I've seen a host of t-shirts our females are wearing that are quite shocking and inappropriate.

Let me give a few examples.

One t-shirt said 'if you are rich, I'm your bitch'.

Another said, 'skinny bitch'.

By the way, the girl was not skinny,

she had bulges coming out of the t-shirt,

and she was holding a little girl's hand.

This could have been her sister, daughter, or a little friend,

but this was not something the little gal pal should have seen when she looked at this adult.

This was not a good example to this young girl.

Another t-shirt said, 'Phat Bitch',

in other words, designer negativity.

I know, it sells, but what is it saying, and what does it represent.

And another, I'll never forget my first (picture of a joystick),

of course, that was intended to be taken in a certain way.

it wasn't talking about Atari or play station.
I was told of another that said,
'I've got killer p%$$# (like the cat)' **Really!!**

Back in the day, killer meant something totally different,
but today, ladies, to refer to your private gems as the killer,
and to advertise it on your chest,
people can take that negative statement negatively,
meaning you're full of STD's or AIDS or positively negative,
meaning that you think your private gem is 'soooo good'.
Well, if the readers think it might be 'sooo good',
then someone is going to want to try it out,
but maybe not who you want it to be.
When I say someone,
I do mean male or female because you are advertising it to the world,
and in the world,
there are all types of lifestyles reading your advertisement,
on your t-shirt.

Quiet as it's kept, ladies, our body is God's temple,
and it is supposed to be saved for marriage,
but certainly, it is not to be advertised like merchandise for sale.

'Tasty', 'hot to trot',
and 'money talks' are light weight compared to some others.
My question for you is **'What does your t-shirt say?**

Ladies and young girls you need to be careful of what you are advertising on your chest.

Remember that this is the very first of a first impression,
no one has talked to you, but they have already 'read you'.

People will 'read you' and they will believe you.
And they will try to take you up on your words.

You'll get mad and say,
'How dare you approach me in that way!',
or 'Oh, no he didn't!', 'Who does he think he is?'
or 'What does he think I am?'
And they may be looking at you confused because the answer will be,
well, your t-shirt said, 'Try me', so........

Question: how are we to stop our boys and men from calling women bitches and
freaks when females advertise themselves as bitches and freaks on their t-shirts?
The ladies will be the first to get mad when someone calls them this.
It's just liked the nigger concept.

Black people are always calling each other niggers
but let a white person or any other race say it to us, we go off.
'How dare you approach me in that way!',
or 'Oh no they didn't', 'Who do they think they are?'

What is your label, what is your advertisement?
what does your t-shirt say?

If you are going to wear words on your chest,
why can't you wear 'the word'?
A positive word is better than a negative word.
Two words can teach a lesson.
'Jesus saves!'
That's a great t-shirt.

Here are some examples of some positive t-shirts,
how about 'Woman of God' or 'Body by God',
'God's Gym', 'No weapon formed against me shall prosper',

'Blessed and highly favored, 'Romans 10:9' or 'John 3:2',

'Jesus loves you and me', or 'I'm a believer,

even Shrek fans can identify with this one.'

Females, please, change your advertisement of yourself.

One thing I want to point out is that whether they are saved or not I have seen very few males wearing a t-shirt labeling themselves with a negative name or advertising their buns or prowess.

I did see a young man wearing a t-shirt that says,

'I'm Rick James bitch.' Now, either he's talking negatively to a female or he is speaking of another relationship w/Rick James, not to be advertised.

I know there might be a few 'Magic Stick' t-shirts out there,

but guys the same rule applies. Even 50-Cent should be wearing a t-shirt that says, 'Jesus Saves.' Jesus saved his life.

he was shot 9 times and is here to tell the story,

but the favor God has given him could be used in a more positive way.

If 50-cent promoted a t-shirt that said, 'Jesus saved me',

all of the young folks would buy it.

G-Unit could represent God's Unit.

A t-shirt is not necessary to wear the armor of God,

but if you are going to wear a t-shirt with words that people will read on you,

let it be a positive reading.

Carry yourselves with dignity; don't put yourself out there to be a target.

When you advertise your body, ladies,

men will be tempted to try you according to what you advertise,

because your t-shirt said you are what you are, and it is what it is.

And another thing,

for those single ladies singing 'I have my t-shirt and my panties on,

do yourself a favor, go get the rest of your clothes and put them on too,

or you will soon wish you had your flannel pajamas and a coat when you see how your life might be jacked up behind a one-night stand booty call, std, aids or pregnancy.

It's like playing Russian roulette.
It only takes one bullet to kill you.
It only takes one 'one-night stand' to jack up your life.
Cover it up ladies until its time with the man God has appointed for you.

Let's change our advertisement to show that we are 'Dressed by God'.
My T-shirt says Birthright; I have the right to be blessed. God Bless you!

Visions

Unfinished

I don't know nothing 'bout birthing no babies
I don't know enough 'bout burying some dead stuff either
But if I could bury some dead stuff
And take the tough with the rough
I would have enough room to birth a few of my babies
Works created from gifts that only God gave me

The babies I need to birth are not delivered from the womb
They do not necessarily need their own room
They will not cry out loud or need a diaper change
They won't need to breastfeed, but need nurturing just the same
When my babies are birthed, you will remember my name
Its an unsigned contract, but its kingdom just the same

I tarry but cannot deliver my babies prematurely
When I pray and I trust, I speak life to them, surely
My babies are not a product of human sperm
These gifts need me to carry them to full term
Great visions, my babies, they, don't come cheap,
To bless for the kingdom, I must make my babies leap

By God, what is unfinished is already finished
He's just waiting for me to grow into it.

Vision Approved

I woke from the dream, I Shouted Halleluiah
Praise God; Glory to your name
In the dream, I knew of information
Very important, that I found
The titles appeared in bold black letters
And the explanation of the

Words to follow appeared, not bolded
In smaller print, with dates and dollar amounts
I cracked the case. I told my boss, who was a
Woman, small, sweet and kind about the information.
To her this was important
She came and told me that because of the information

That I produced, the bold black letters
And words in small print, with dates and dollar amounts
There was going to be a breakthrough
They were going to release he information
My breakthrough was about to be released. Halleluiah!
It was a sign from God
To continue forth with my writing

My titles in bold and words in smaller print
Each title dated and worth
Dollars!
Go forth and release
Release and unleash my season
Release the breakthrough
You are about to be rewarded
Because you are glorifying Him!
Thank you, God, for the dream.

Word Acapella

I do not want to get too deep; can you remember what you've heard
When I read to you my rhymes or minister my written word
It'd be fine if I had a piano to back up my spoken song
But if the message were of God would acapella be so wrong
I could add a bounce to my praise, do a dance as my words came out

But the act wouldn't be correct for you to know what I'm talking about
I could tell you to clap to this, I could tell you to stomp your feet
I'd rather ask you to hear and receive for a word that you will repeat
Using wisdom, you'll learn to receive, when being given a word of the Lord
The word delivered should help you believe, in our God and His just rewards

It's so easy to be entertained, if not amused, then you tend to reject Him
God's word is food for your brain, you must learn to show you respect Him
Other acts have a musical need, I need silence to get your attention
It's your soul my words help to feed, as you're steered to divine intervention
Here's a word and it's not dressed up, it's a thought that your destined to keep

It instructs you to lift Him up, and to praise Him even in sleep
I don't want to get too deep, so you know just what you've heard
When reciting my poems to you or delivering a spoken word
It'd be fine If I had a guitar or some music with spoken song
It is important you learn to receive, worship our God, and praise the Lord!

Word Up!

My Million Is Waiting for Me

I know that my million is waiting for me
My mind has a heavenly vision
I'm dreaming and planning and building you see
And all this was God's great decision
I know I will make it, my goal to succeed
With ambition divine and so rare
I'll produce and promote and give Jesus the praise
When I am a millionaire
My dominant gift always on my mind
Though my dreams have not yet been fulfilled
But I have decided to waste no more time
It is time that my land I will till
I'll not be discouraged by doubters of me
Catch your dream and pursue your own mission
I know that my million is waiting for me
I represent God in my vision
I do not have to tell you what my vision is
Or how I will earn my first million
With faith and not fear I will preserver
As I'm fruitful and taking dominion
To do kingdom business you have to believe this
There's more to life than you expect
Step out with your faith and step up with your praise
And you'll see more than just a paycheck
If your vision is plain, you should never refrain
From putting your vision in view
Your ideas will be driven from what the Lord's given
Replenish and then you'll subdue
Expand on your vision and make your fruition
And try to succeed if you dare
It is your destiny that you walk in, you'll see
As you label yourself, millionaire
When I make my first million, I will not depend on

The million I've already made
My thoughts on the table will show me as able
Ensuring new money is paid
I see this so clearly my plan is not nearly
As false as you think it to be
God will get the glory as I tell the story
My million is waiting for me

Call Me the Owner

I am the CEO, I am Head -Saint -in -Charge
You can call me the owner; I will be living large
Yes, I will brag and boast, even if I struggle
Expect some pain to gain, I plan to profit double
My mentor taught me well; he taught me how to plan
To profit with my skills, and answer to demand
No more will I be drained of knowledge, skills and talent
Resources I have gained will make success apparent
No boss will tell me when, though I will work all hours
To make my business grow, for assets create power
I will not go alone, but to the top I'll take it
Whoever follows me, will prosper not forsake it
I realize my worth, converting skills to dollars
God gave us all we need; We've been his faithful scholars
I'm so excited Lord because it's in the making
Now free from puppeteers, so now it is no more faking
No longer grinning or bearing, while hating what I make
My pay is not my worth, one third is what they take
I will be self-employed, I do not plan to fail
I know I will succeed because my God prevails
My life has been corrected with Faith & Strength in Christ
In Him we do all things and recognize birthright
I have the right to be blessed as I go forth with my plans
So, you can call me the owner as I inherit my land

NOW!

Teddy Bears and Balloons

In the neighborhoods we travel, whether day or night,
We are constantly reminded of a loss of life
Stabbing pain in our hearts, river tears in our eyes,
Teddy Bears and balloons, we have come to despise
Teddy bears and balloons mark a place of death;
Where a relative or friend took their last breath

Lit candles, and vigils, clothes showered with tears,
Sad memorials, confirming the worst of our fears
Mothers crying their hearts out; Dads hurting and mad,
Now a total neighborhood made extremely sad
As they grieve for a life unexpectedly killed,
Hearts broken, shattered dreams, futures unfulfilled
Some never had a chance to enjoy their life.

Some never had a chance to give their lives to Christ
Some never had a chance to pray and repent,
Some begged for their life but murder was sent
Some victims died young, and some died older,
Each death so senseless, some died like soldiers

It's death in the streets, but the streets aren't killing.
The murderer is ignorance amongst the living
Meant to represent good, now it stands for dead,
Teddy bears and balloons placed somewhere ahead
On a pole, in the park, at the corner of a street,
It's a place of final breath, causing us to weep.
What is the resolution for murder in the streets?
We must pray for change, and not accept defeat

A prayer contribution doesn't cost a dime,

Takes a little of your time, covers yours and mines
We must pray for our homes, and our family,
Pray for safety for neighbors and communities
Promoting prayer is worth a shot, it may stop a bullet.
Someone's finger on a trigger might decide not to pull it
When we travel the city, it'd be great to see flowers,
Or something that reflects God's positive power

Not an act of violence or an act of a coward
Put your mind on the future, not a victim's last hour
Teddy Bears and Balloons fill your world with gloom,
People dying in vain and they're dying too soon
So, let's pray without ceasing, against death and doom.
Stop the violence and need for Teddy Bears and balloons

Can I Take a Walk?

My 14-year-old grandson asked 'Grandma, can I take a walk around the corner?

It was 6:00 pm, in my neighborhood. He's from the hood, but not this hood.

Me: 'Uh....'

The thoughts in my mind at the time was like a movie of the last years events

Of George Floyd murdered unnecessarily by the police,

Of sons killed being in the wrong place at the wrong time,

Of Trayvon Martin being shot in his hoodie in 2012, my grandson wears hoodies

Of black boys shot dead because they were afraid and ran

Of young boys being bullied by strangers because they know they're not from 'around here.'

Harassed by their own peers, the ignorant, uneducated, or racists that are up to no good,

Stopped by cops for no reason, liars justifying brutality, shootings, or beatings

The concern for our black sons returning home has grown.

You see, all lives matter, but if boys are killed and don't become men, there's no reproduction

My grandson is normally my protector, but I had to protect him, I couldn't let him go alone.

My fear that should not have been, was if I wasn't with him, would he return?

I wanted my grandson to come back home, so therefore I did not let him leave.

My Grandson: 'Grandma, can I take a walk around the corner?'

Me: 'No, grandson. It's 6:00 o'clock at night.'

B.O.U.N.D- The Story of Angel
Blessings Obstructed by Unhealthy Negative Devices

Blocked arteries stop the heart from functioning and blood from flowing correctly.

When you are bound by issues, people, places, and things,

it's just like having blocked arteries.

Your heart cannot function properly if your arteries are blocked,

your mind cannot function properly if you are bound with issues that are holding you back from

being the person God wants you to be.

This is the story of Angel, From Being Bound to Being Blessed

Angel was living in a state of bondage.

She was bound by her past issues,

painful situations and abusive relationships

She traveled from one state of bondage to another,

tripping, dipping, and slipping.

Her mind was like a bank,

where she deposited the hurts and painful experiences along the way,

never making withdrawals to clear her focus.

For Angel, there was always that false sense of security that the next trip would be the last trip,

Each rejection and hurt started another search for FUN and love.

What she didn't realize is that she should not have been looking!

Angel held on to her low self-esteem,

accepting the negativity, she received

Accepting unions, not all relational,

accepting abuses, some generational

Accepting death, some devastational,

Consuming drugs, some recreational,

Nursing alcoholics, dancing with adulterers,

excusing the abusers, and living with accusers,

No one was worthy, but she didn't know her worth,
she thought, this was the life she was destined to live.
Not really loving herself, but always trying to save someone else,
instead of seeking, always offering help.
Finally, Angel was led to a man, Jesus Christ,
What she learned began to change her life,
but she wasn't all in, yet.

Living wound up and bound up for years,
how could she just change her ways?
After suffering such heaviness in her days.
Searching for happiness was like a smoking gun when all she wanted was to have
a little FUN
But the fun never lasted, and it always hurt at the end,
a repetitive cycle, again and again
Angel's mind was not sound, less up, mostly down,
what was the root cause that caused her to be bound?

By living this way, she continued to hurt others and be hurt,
including God, who knew and loved her first.
She continued to compromise her seed,
and her actions never satisfied her need
To be made whole.
Angel finally stopped putting God upon the shelf and asked the Lord,
'what am I doing to myself?'
Angel started praying, reading the bible,
and hearing the word to which she became liable.

She came across a scripture Matthew 6:33
the word didn't say to seek you or seek me,
it said something that she would find later to be true
seek ye first the kingdom of God and his righteousness and these things shall be
added unto you.

Angel realized that, she had been doing it backwards.
She wanted to get it right, going forward.

Problem is that just like Angel,

most of us were not seeking the kingdom first,

we're seeking the kingdom later.

We are bound to be bound by something if we don't know about the kingdom of God and Jesus

Christ, our Lord and Savior.

Angel kept reading, and found other scriptures

Psalm 30:5 the word says for his anger endure but a moment,

in his favor is life, weeping may endure for a night,

but JOY cometh in the mourning.

Angel was seeking FUN first,

bound in state of disobedience and using anger instead of prayer which created many

grievances. The more Angel read, the more she learned.

Psalm 27:4 says, wait on the Lord, be of good courage,

and he shall strengthen thine heart: The word is giving the instruction, and the benefit part.

Before accepting Christ, Angel was discouraged.

The word WAIT was not in her vocabulary.

Angel wanted to be loved, and not hurt, she wanted to function with a clear mind and a

functional heart. But there was a man, Jesus Christ.

In the word, Jesus explains his love for all man. When a son of the kingdom understands the love

of Jesus, he will know how to love a woman, his rib, correctly.

Angel discovered the root cause of her bondage and issues she carried, once she read this next

scripture:

Isaiah 54:17 says No weapon formed against me shall prosper.

Angel realized she had called upon and invited in the very weapons that she was praying not to

be formed against her. Angel learned to pray for healing and deliverance.

Angels quest for Christ became consistent, she no longer struggled or was resistant of the power

of God. She fought stronger and harder against the devil's devices.

The more that she accepted who she was in Christ,
the more the chains that bound her fell off, link by link.
She absorbed the word, and she prayed.
Angel finally realized who she was, and who God had destined for her to be.
Angel has gone from being bound to being blessed.

There is only one man that she needs and that is Jesus Christ.
Angel is now waiting on her Boaz,
and she is no longer looking as she expects to be found.
The Beginning!

Why am I the B.O.M.B.?
(Blessed Overcomer Manifested to Believe)

Why am I the BOMB?
I'm glad you asked.
A soldier in God's army, I'm being trained by His word
Finding shelter in the trenches of His arms, I am protected,
Delving deeper into the kingdom of God,
I am on the road to the kingdom of Heaven.

Why am I the BOMB?
As a warrior under His shield, I am sheltered from the enemy's fire.
As a restored woman of God, I found courage to encourage
In the face of fear, His word says Fear not!

Isaiah 41:10 says 'Fear not! I am thy God, I am with you, I will strengthen and help you'
I seek refuge in the trenches of the word and His presence

Why am I the BOMB?
The word has let me know I am More than a Conqueror
*Romans 8:37 says, in '**all these things** we are more than conquerors through him that loved us'.*
I am a Survivor of trials, tribulations, setbacks, and disappointments
I am a child, daughter, sister, mother, aunt, mentor, friend, & woman of God
In a cold world, cold house, cold heart, I have provided warmth to many.
Because He loved me first, I've loved hard with my heart, for some until death, did we part

Why am I the BOMB?
I can walk proud and stand tall
I am my Father's child, and His name I will call

Why am I the BOMB?
Psalm 139:14 says 'I will praise thee; for I am fearfully and wonderfully made: marvelous are thy works; and that my soul knoweth right well'.

Yes, my soul knoweth right well that I need Jesus

I was formed as a woman from one of Adams Ribs, with the ability to produce many things

I can birth babies, ideas, businesses, and ministries

I am a child, daughter, sister, mother, aunt, mentor, friend, & woman of God

Designed by God, I am fearfully and wonderfully made.

Again, you ask, 'Why am I the bomb?' Because He raised me that way.

Philippians 4:13 says 'I can do all things through Christ which strengthens me.'

(Therefore, without Christ, I am limited.)

He is the leader of my army, I need to follow his direction

Isaiah 54:17 says 'No weapon that is formed against me shall prosper;

and every tongue that shall rise against thee in judgment thou shalt condemn.

This is the heritage of the servants of the Lord, and their righteousness is of me, saith the Lord.'

***I am the BOMB**, because I have inherited the right for the Lord to cover and protect me,*

with His righteousness! The Lord has got my back.

2 Corinthians 10:4 says

'For the weapons of our warfare are not carnal,

but mighty through God to the pulling down of strong holds'

I am training in the trenches, but not with guns, knives, sticks or chains,

God's word is my sword and shield,

My testimony is that He has changed me,

pulled some strong holds off me so that I can set other captives free

Fighting on the frontline, I am TNT, Training in the Trenches, Ms. Dynamite!

Because of HIS light, am no longer in darkness, by the Power of His might

I am the BOMB!

2 Chronicles 20:15

'And he said, Hearken ye, all Judah,

and ye inhabitants of Jerusalem, and thou king Jehoshaphat,

Thus saith the Lord unto you,

Be not afraid nor dismayed by reason of this great multitude;

for the battle is not yours, but God's.'
I don't have to fight the enemy alone;
I have God who surrounds me in my battle. Who's bad??

Why am I the bomb? *Because of Him.*

Matthew 6:33 KJV
33 But seek ye first the kingdom of God, and his righteousness;
and all these things shall be added unto you.
I learned what I should be searching for in this life, while training in the trenches

Philippians 1:21
For to me to live is Christ, and to die is gain.
In the battle within, I had to die to myself, had to surrender to win
Lost more of me to gain more of Him, just as Christ died for our sins

Ephesians 6:10-18
Finally, my brethren, be strong in the Lord, and in the power of his might.
Put on the whole armor of God, that ye may be able to stand against the wiles of the devil.
I may undress at night and redress in the morning, but the armor of God is always upon me
*Because I am Training in the Trenches, and **I am the BOMB!***
Blessed Overcomer Manifested to Believe!

(R.I.P.) Rag in Progress
Poem

There have been times when I've been used
Just like a worn-out rag

First pretty, in a package, still wrapped in the bag
Folded, nice and neat, just waiting to be sprung
As soon as I was wet, after first use, I was done

Being spread where no rag cared to be spread
Soaked in unfit waters, not fit for my threads

Wiping dirt, mud and spoils, folks could care less
Taking my cloth for granted let the rag clean the mess
Let the rag get it, that's what the rag is there for
Such a Brawny rag used to clean your mess and more

I am tattered and worn; my soft hands now rough
Yet you've squeezed, wrung me out, still I've sparkled your stuff

Yet you use me to clean up your same nasty mess
From the spots to the mud this old rag does it best

They say, 'use that rag, her! She'll clean up our spills
She does it so good, no one cares how she feels'

Will I clean your house in the morning with Dawn?
Wipe your spots with Joy while you sit on the lawn

Will I team with Mr. Clean and make it all 'Spic and Span'?
Will I flow with your Tide, you refusing your hand?

Well suppose I am Zesty and lemony fresh
When I tell you I'll no longer clean up your mess

I'm a righteous rag, and I do feel quite worn
But I have wiped my last spill and my torn threads are gone

As a new rag in progress, I'll be better not broken
God is cleansing my soul for to me he has spoken
I will call on the Lord as He's cleansing my soul
He's the quicker picker upper, I'll let Him take control

(R.I.P)
· Rag In Progress- The Play
By : Tree Pears

Cast of Characters

DEMOND

ANGEL

NARRATOR

LYNITA

SISTER MAYDELL

THE WOMEN

SISTER CHERYL

PASTOR MIRENSON

CONGREGATION

ACT 1
Scene One

Scene takes place at Angel's home as she arrives from work.

Angel walks in the door, arriving home from work, looking worn out and tired. She puts down her briefcase and looks at her husband, Demond.

Demond is sitting in his fat leather chair, with everything he needs on the table to the right of him; his cigarettes, his 6 pack of malt liquor, some TOP rolling paper with a bag of weed and remote controls for everything, the TV, the DVD, and the ceiling fan.

As soon as Angel comes in, she notices right away the smell of cigarette smoke, and malt liquor funk. She immediately looks for the can of air freshener sitting by Demond's foot.

Demond: *Hey Angel honey, what cha looking for?*

Angel: *I'm looking for the air freshener, what do you think, it stinks in here.*

Demond: *What 'cha mean, honey?*

Angel: *You know darn well what I mean. You been smoking up in here and drinking that stinking malt liquor.*

Demond: *What? You mean these cans? They were from last week! (Demond looks like he is lying.)*

Angel: *Demond please, you tell that lie every week. This place smells like fresh cigarettes, and you know I can't stand that smell, my nostrils are ruined from breathing in secondhand smoke. If those cans of Hurricane were from last week, how come it's still 3 cans that ain't opened?*

Demond: *Damn, girl, who you work for, the FBI, CIA or Dick frickin Tracey, which one?*

Angel: *(Looks at Demond with a smirk of disgust and walks over to the kitchen area, noticing the dishes still in the sink).*

Angel: *'Damn, Demond, couldn't you straighten up some in here?*

Demond: *Oh yeah, I was gonna get it, just leave it. I'll take care of it, later. What's for dinner?*

Narrator: *Demond grabs a cigarette and acts like he's going outside to smoke.*

Angel: *Demond! You could have had dinner ready already! How is it that I work all day, and then come in here, and you're sitting your lazy ass in the chair in front of the TV all day? Like somebody's paying you to watch it. You know the dishes need to be done and dinner needs to be cooked. Haven't I worked hard enough already today?*

Demond: *No, you still have to fix my dinner, woman! Oh, here's the electric and the water bill, and the phone bill, they all came today. You better hurry up and pay them; we can't be without no water or electric up in here. (Hands Angel the bills).*

Angel: *(Snatches the bills from Demond with a frown). I wonder how much less the bills would be if it was just me living here?*

Demond: *(Speaks drunkenly) Angel, honey, did you stop at the store on your way home? We need a loaf of bread and some toilet paper. (Laughingly) Oh yeah babe, I need some tokens and twenty dollars. I have a doctor's appointment this week.*
Angel: *Yeah, well, what's the twenty dollars for?*

Demond: *Oh, you know, just in case I get hungry while I'm waiting at the doctor's office. (Demond looks into the audience) I got a few hot numbers to play. I hit last week on 526 in the box! I got me a quick 40.00, but she doesn't know though. (Demond laughs out loud).*

Angel: *(Shakes her head) I'm exhausted, and what do I look like, Wells Fargo? And here you are sitting in here, drunk again!*

Demond: *(Responds drunkenly) I'm not drunk Angel, I'm just tired, that's all.*

Angel: *Yeah, that's how I know you're drunk. You always say you're tired when you're drunk. (Walks away from Demond and goes in the dining room. She looks in the mirror over the buffet and studies herself.)*

Narrator: *Angel is a pretty woman who could be really beautiful, but right now she looks worn down and worn out. Her clothes are an outfit straight out of the 80s; pullover shirt, polyester pants, run over shoes, and surely, she needs a new hairdo, and some make up.*

Angel: *(Says out loud) I feel like a worn-out dish rag! I'm so tired. (Continues talking to herself in the mirror, as if she were talking to God). I am tired of everything. I am tired of this life. I am tired of working and paying bills. I am tired of him! (She points into the living room at Demond) and I don't even want to come home. (Begins to cry). Oh Lord, this can't be the way that I spend the rest of my life.*

Angel: *(Looks down on the table, sees the track and the CD that was handed to her from Pastor Mirenson at the Church of Grace & Peace. She picks them up and turns to go upstairs when Demond stops her in her tracks).*

Demond: *Where do you think you're going, woman?*

Angel: *I am going upstairs in my room to rest!*

Demond: *Oh no you're not! Not until you fix my dinner. You're trying to get up there to listen to that bullcrap from that crazy hollering, jumping and shouting, money stealing church! They ain't nothing but a bunch of crooks. The Pastor is always looking at me like I'm a happy meal! They're always taking up a collection, and where is it going? Always trying to convince you on how you need God. I am your God and your savior, Baby. I am the best thing you ever had. Remember, I made your Booty Call bounce! I will deliver you right here, baby, right here.*

Demond: *(Grabs his crotch) Now hurry up and fix your God something to eat!*

Angel: *(Smiled devilishly) Ok, honey. (Looking at the audience as Demond is distracted) Hmmm, I could put a little rat poison in the food. Oh Lord, I am so sorry. Please forgive me, I repent.*

Demond: *(Sits back down, and pops open another 16-ounce can of Hurricane malt liquor, and hollers at the TV).*

Demond: *Run nigga, run! Get him! Get him! Get him*

Scene Two
The scene takes place in Angel's kitchen.

Narrator: Angel just finished cleaning the kitchen floor and the phone rings. It's her daughter.

Angel: Hey, Lynita,

Lynita: Hey, mom. How are you?

Angel: I'm good. Where's my grandbabies?

Lynita: They upstairs, playing.

Angel: Tell them I love them.

Lynita: You sound tired.

Angel: Yeah baby, I am tired.

Lynita: Where is Demond and how is he?

Angel: Demond's in the living room. Can't you hear him coughing and choking? But I bet you he won't stop smoking. He's in there hollering at the TV, watching Smackdown, or as I call it 'Men in Tights.' Lynita, I need to sit down for a minute. Let me call you back.

Angel: (Turns on the TV to find the ministry channel and Joyce Meyers is on. She is teaching on Proverbs 31 verses 10 - 31, a scripture about being a virtuous woman.) (A voice in the background is reading the scripture as Angel reflects on it.)

[10] [c] *A wife of noble character who can find? She is worth far more than rubies.*

[11] *Her husband has full confidence in her and lacks nothing of value.*

[12] *She brings him good, not harm, all the days of her life.*

[13] *She selects wool and flax and works with eager hands.*

[14] *She is like the merchant ships, bringing her food from afar.*

[15] *She gets up while it is still dark; she provides food for her family and portions for her servant girls.*

¹⁶ *She considers a field and buys it; out of her earnings she plants a vineyard.*

¹⁷ *She sets about her work vigorously; her arms are strong for her tasks.*

¹⁸ *She sees that her trading is profitable, and her lamp does not go out at night.*

¹⁹ *In her hand she holds the distaff and grasps the spindle with her fingers.*

²⁰ *She opens her arms to the poor and extends her hands to the needy.*

²¹ *When it snows, she has no fear for her household; for all of them are clothed in scarlet.*

²² *She makes coverings for her bed; she is clothed in fine linen and purple.*

²³ *Her husband is respected at the city gate, where he takes his seat among the elders of the land.*

²⁴ *She makes linen garments and sells them and supplies the merchants with sashes.*

²⁵ *She is clothed with strength and dignity; she can laugh at the days to come.*

²⁶ *She speaks with wisdom, and faithful instruction is on her tongue.*

²⁷ *She watches over the affairs of her household and does not eat the bread of idleness.*

²⁸ *Her children arise and call her blessed; her husband also, and he praises her:*

²⁹ *"Many women do noble things, but you surpass them all."*

³⁰ *Charm is deceptive, and beauty is fleeting; but a woman who fears the LORD is to be praised.*

³¹ *Give her the reward she has earned, and let her works bring her praise at the city gate.*

Angel: *(With tears in her eyes, she begins to talk to the Lord). Lord, I don't know you, but I know I need you. I need help, Lord. I know I am a good woman, but I'm caught in a trap. I know I deserve better, Lord. Lord, this marriage is not what I wanted it to be. Lord, my soul is being abused, verbally, mentally, and emotionally! Demond's issues are killing me. I can't take this anymore. I don't feel like a virtuous woman, Lord. I need help. Help me, please! (She breaks down and cries).*

Narrator: *In the background, Demond is still hollering at the TV. He's hollering, "Shoot that nigga!" Angel grabs her track and Sermon CD off of the table and walks past Demond, with tears in her eyes, and up the steps to her room. Even though Angel was paying all of the bills, somehow, she had the smallest bedroom in the house.*

Demond: *(Hollers) Hey honey, what's wrong? Why are you crying? You got onion juice in your eyes again? Ha-ha-ha-ha-ha.*

Scene Three

Fade to next scene, as Demond chokes on a cigarette while he islaughing at his own joke.

Angel: *(Hollers down the steps)* Demond! Stop smoking in the house, doggonnit!

Demond: *(Quickly puts out the cigarette, trying to hide it, and hollers back to Angel)* I ain't smoking in here. That's from outside!

Narrator: Demond shushes the audience.

ACT 2
Scene One

Characters
Angel
Sister Maydell
The women at the meeting

Scene begins with Angel walking outside towards the church.

Angel decided to take a walk after Demond had pissed her off. As she walked down the street past Pastor Mirenson's church, The Church of Grace and Peace, she was drawn in by the syrupy voice of a woman speaking, who was ministering about becoming strong in the Lord, and bringing yourself out of bondage. Angel walked in and sat down in the back of the church.

Sister Maydell: Welcome, young lady. What is your name?

Angel: *(Answers sadly)* Angel, Angel McEvers.

Sister Maydell: Angel, come on up here. Don't sit all the way back there. We won't bite you. Welcome to our women's ministry meeting. I am Sister Maydell Do-well.

Sister Maydell: *(Says to the women)* Y'all turn around and welcome Angel up in here. Give her some of that Grace, peace, and love.

The women: Welcome Angel, welcome. Glad you could make it. Don't be scared, come on in.

Sister Maydell: *It is so important for us women to realize who we are in Christ and get to know Him, so that we can be healed, delivered, set free. Many of you are living in relationships that you're not too proud of. You're being abused and keeping it a secret. Whether it is physically, mentally, or emotionally, it's tearing you down. What's worse is a form of self-abuse because you are choosing to stay in it. Some of you are walking around saying you feel like a 'worn-out rag.'*

The women: *(Speak in agreement, like in a regular sermon).*

Angel: *(Laughed) Hey, that's my saying.*

Sister Maydell: *Baby, it's time you graduate from being a 'worn-out rag' to 'a rag in progress.' Just like a work in progress, the foundation is laid, and it just improves from there. Well, so does a rag in progress. The rag, a righteously anointed woman of God, is someone who takes a stand for her own life. You may have a broken spirit, be broken down, or broken hearted. The more you pick up the bible and receive a Word, connect with other strong women and ministers of God, your life and attitude will change. You will begin to develop a 'no more nonsense, no more drama, and no more abuse attitude.' You will also develop a relationship with Jesus Christ.*

The women: *Amen, Mother. I know that's right!*

Angel: *(Starts to tear up, but she knew Sister Maydell was right).*

Sister Maydell: *Babies, you are all here for a reason tonight. I want you to continue joining us for these meetings, so I can help you and we can help each other. At one time, I was in the same place that some of you are now. When I reached out for God's help, He took my hand and He never let it go. I've been through drug addiction and been delivered. I used to have low self-esteem and booty call drama. I have started all over several times, but through the power of God, I have become a righteously anointed woman of God, and I am here for you. I am out of time. Sister Cheryl, can you please close us out in prayer?*

Sister Cheryl: *Father God, in the name of Jesus. Please give us traveling mercies. Cover us on the way home and in our homes Lord. Let the healing begin and keep us under your wing, in Jesus's name I pray, Amen.*

Narrator: *Angel stood up to go and turned to leave with so much on her mind.*

Sister Maydell: *Angel. Wait a minute, baby. I want to talk with you. First, can you fill this information out so we can keep in touch with you? Remember, we have service on Sunday at 11:00 am, and bible study every Tuesday night at 7:00 pm.*

Narrator: Sister Maydell visits Angel at her home and yells for her at the front door in a motherly voice.

Sister Maydell: Angel!

Angel: Come on in Sister Maydell. (Angel is sitting on the sofa, holding her head in her hands).

Sister Maydell: Angel, why are you sitting here looking like you got an anchor on your bottom lip? If you're this sad, why ain't ya trying to do something to change your situation? Look at you, you're working like a slave every day, then you get up and go to work. You're wearing yourself out! When are you going to rest? You just got out of the hospital, and your diabetes is out of control. You can barely breath, inhaling all this secondhand smoke all of the time. Half the time, you smell like malt liquor and you don't even drink! Angel, every time I see you, you're just crying, crying, crying, crying, boo hooing, and did I mention crying?

Angel: (Starts crying again).

Sister Maydell: You need to start investing some 'positivity' into your own life, instead of cleaning up everyone else's mess all of the time.

Angel: But Demond!

Sister Maydell: What?! The heck with Demond! Demond is an ass butt. Forgive me, Lord. It's time for you to think about yourself for a change. If you are looking for a change in your life, nobody can do it like God! He did it for me, and He can do it for you. Honey, you've got to give it to Him. Let go and let God. Just ask Him to 'Do It!'

Angel: Sister Maydell, it wasn't like this when we first got married. I thought we would be such a happy couple, but we don't even like the same things. I am just learning how to pray, but I am still the only one praying. It seems all he's interested in is sitting in front of the TV with the remote control, smoking his cigarettes, and drinking his malt liquor. That stuff stinks! They put that stuff in our neighborhoods, so people, mostly our men can afford a cheap high. It ain't nothing but liquid crack. It makes you look stupid, talk stupid, and act stupid. Did I say it stinks? He drinks it all day and I've got a name for each one. Hurricane, that's a natural disaster. St. Ides, beware the Ides in the hood. Old English 800, that's furniture polish. Steel Reserve 211, that's scrap metal. Oh, and Colt 45, well, put a gun to your head, why don't you. It's all a trick of the enemy to steal, kill, and destroy our men. I see other women with what appears to be great marriages. Why can't I have one? Demond always brags that he never cheated on me, but Sister Maydell, I feel cheated, gypped, hoodwinked, bamboozled. In order for him to love me better, he needs to love himself better, so that he can be there for me, to be my strength, my backup, and my protection. I feel like I am just wasting my words, my breath, and my time. It's been a very stressful relationship. Therefore, I'm always crying.

Sister Maydell: *(She puts her arms around Angel)* Angel, you never know what problems are in other couple's marriages, or in another woman's life, but if you ask God for what you want and pray continually, you will see that He answers prayers because He is a way maker. Go ahead, just ask Him.'

Narrator: *Old spiritual plays 'Lord, Do it' by: James Cleveland as Sister Maydell is hugging Angel and ministering to her. She is showing her scriptures in the Bible. Fade out.*

Scene Three

Suppose I feel zesty and lemony fresh and tell you I'll no longer clean up your mess.
Scene begins in Angel's house: Angel is in the house with the Gospel music playing softly.
Demond Sitting in the living room with an attitude. Angel is spraying air freshener heavy, with the windows open, and Shekinah Glory is singing Stomp on the devil's head. Angel is stomping around the living room, as she is preparing to go to church. Demond hollers to Angel.

Demond: *Angel, will you stop spraying that stuff in here!*

Angel: *If you can keep smoking the stuff I hate to smell, I can spray this air freshener that you hate to smell.*

Demond: *And wait a minute! Where did you get that outfit from? That ain't nothing you normally wear, and why you got on that makeup? When did you have enough money to get your hair done like that? You been holding out on me, woman? Are you sure you're going to church?*

Narrator: *Angel is still strutting and stomping, looking at herself in the mirror.*

Demond: *(Starts to throw a tantrum) Why are you smiling like a Cheshire cat? What the hell is going on here? And turn that 'stomp' music off before I stomp on* *your head! Why it got to be all loud? You trying to let the neighbors hear it.?*

Angel: *(Still stomping and praising the Lord) Whew, Halleluiah! Stomp on the devil's head! Let the neighbors hear it, you're worthy Lord. Glory, I learned how to praise Him. My God is an awesome God, he reigns, and He rocks. Thank you, Lord. Thank you, Jesus.*

Demond: *Now cut that out!*

Angel: *No, Demond. You know what I'm about to cut out? You, Demond! We are not now, and we have never been equally yoked, since the beginning of this marriage. I think that I am finally tired of putting up with your crap. You know, they always say, you don't have to tell a fool when they are tired. Well, I've been a fool long enough, and I am tired of being tired.*

I am no longer going to be afraid to speak up for my life. You are draining the life out of me, and I have learned through the power of prayer that I can claim my life back. I am no longer sleeping with the enemy, and right now, the enemy is living in you.

Demond: *What the hell are you talking about woman?*

Angel: *I am talking about getting you, the hell, out of my life! Demond, you've got to go!*

Demond: *What? I ain't going nowhere!*

Angel: *I am divorcing you. You've got to go.*

Demond: *I ain't signing nothing! I'll contest it. You're my wife. Oh, so you all holier than thou now, huh?*

Angel: *Demond, no, I am not 'holier than thou', but I learned that I could strive to be holier. If you don't want to change, so be it. But I don't have to live this way anymore, if I don't want to, and I don't want to anymore. Love don't live here anymore! I need to be able to breathe clean air and smell the flowers while I'm alive. I need to be able to praise God on the daily, and experience heaven here on earth, because it feels good, and it's so satisfying. You may get it eventually, but I'm not waiting on you. You've needed me all this time, but I can no longer be your crutch. I need God, now! I realize it's your demon spirits that has been keeping me bound, and I got to shake them loose, my brother.*

Demond: *(Begins to plead with Angel) Please Angel; is there anything we can do to rectify this situation?*

Angel: *(Shakes her head) I'm sorry Demond. It's too late.*

Narrator: *As the music plays, Demond stands devastated. (Song/Dance) Shake Yourself Loose by: Vickie Winans*

Angel: *(Begins dancing and shouting in the end off of the stage).*

ACT 3
Scene One

Narrator: *Angel stands before the congregation, with her Bible in her hand. Not only is she clothed and dressed in her right mind, but she looks pretty sharp to boot. Angel looks much different than what she looked like 4 months ago. Her hair and her makeup look great, and she has on a fashionable suit, with matching heels, looking like a woman of God, a woman of character, a woman of high self-esteem. She has just finished ministering to the congregation about becoming a Rag in Progress, a Righteously Anointed woman of God that she was destined to be.*

In order to do this, she had to learn how to build a solid foundation, using faith, strength, trust, vision, empowerment, determination, and perseverance. Her divorce is now final.

Pastor Mirenson: *Come on and put your hands together for this awesome woman of God, Sister Angel. I remember when you first walked into this church, now look at God!*

Congregation: *Amen!*

Pastor Mirenson: *Sister Angel will now be ministering to other woman, helping them to break loose from the chains that are keeping them bound. She will be teaching on what's blocking their access to God.*

Demond: *(Sits in the congregation, a broken man. Realizing if he had just listened, he and Angel might still be together. Tears ran down his eyes as he realizes how beautiful Angel is and what a good woman he had but lost.*

Pastor Mirenson: *Desmond, could you come up please? I want to pray for you.*

Sister Maydell: *(Standing by his side, along with other members of the congregation).*

Pastor Mirenson: *Demond, you too can be a man of God, but you need to seek*

God on a daily basis. Learn to study the Word and pray. You could gain your life back, one day at a time, but you must accept the Lord into your heart. The Lord could free you from addictions and demons, with prayer. You can use the same bricks that Angel spoke about to build a solid foundation for your salvation. Look at Angel now, a beautiful woman of God. This time no one can take from her what God has restored. Now let us all pray.

Narrator: *Everyone bows their heads in prayer.*

CPSIA information can be obtained
at www.ICGtesting.com
Printed in the USA
BVHW040201070821
613314BV00008B/211